How Fire is a Story,
Waiting

HOW
FIRE
is a
STORY,
WAITING

poems

MELINDA
PALACIO

TÍA CHUCHA PRESS
LOS ANGELES

Printed in the United States.

ISBN 978-1-882688-44-9

Book Design: Jane Brunette
Cover painting by Margaret Garcia. Used with permission.
Back cover author photo by Daniel Zolinsky

PUBLISHED BY:
Tía Chucha Press
A Project of Tía Chucha's Centro Cultural, Inc.
PO Box 328
San Fernando, CA 91341
www.tiachucha.com

DISTRIBUTED BY:
Northwestern University Press
Chicago Distribution Center
11030 South Langley Avenue
Chicago IL 60628

Tía Chucha Press is the publishing wing of Tía Chucha's Centro Cultural, Inc., a 501 (c) 3 nonprofit corporation. Tía Chucha's Centro Cultural has received funding for this book from the National Endowment for the Arts and individual donors. Other funding for Tía Chucha's Centro Cultural's programming and operations has come from the California Arts Council, Los Angeles County Arts Commission, Los Angeles Department of Cultural Affairs, The California Community Foundation, the Annenberg Foundation, the Weingart Foundation, National Association of Latino Arts and Culture, Ford Foundation, MetLife, Southwest Airlines, the Andy Warhol Foundation for the Visual Arts, the Thrill Hill Foundation, the Middleton Foundation, Center for Cultural Innovation, John Irvine Foundation, Not Just Us Foundation, the Attias Family Foundation, and the Guacamole Fund, among others. Donations have also come from Bruce Springsteen, John Densmore of The Doors, Jackson Browne, Lou Adler, Richard Foos, Gary Stewart, Charles Wright, Adrienne Rich, Tom Hayden, Dave Marsh, Jack Kornfield, Jesus Trevino, David Sandoval, Denise Chávez and John Randall of the Border Book Festival, Luis & Trini Rodríguez, and many more.

Contents

Part 2: Air Carries Her

Part 3: Water Rises South

Part 4: Earth Spins

Para
Maria Victoria Ibarra Gutierrez

Fire

1

How Fire
is a Story,
Waiting

How Fire is a Story, Waiting

My grandmother caught the flame in her thick hands.
Curled fingers made nimble by kaleidoscope embers.
Fire burns hot and cold if you know where to touch it, she said.

I watched the red glow spit and wiggle as it
snaked down the thin timber, a striptease,
born out of the festive sound of a half-filled matchbox.

Through orange windows framed by obsidian eyes, I saw the child she once was.
A little girl who raised herself because her mother had a coughing disease.
Blood on her mother's handkerchief didn't stop her from dreaming.
Maria Victoria was going to be a singer with her deep, cinnamon stick voice.

She watched novelas in the kitchen while waiting for dough to rise.
Her body, heavy with worry for two families and three lifetimes. She tucked
Mariachi dreams under her girdle. Lullabies escaped on mornings
warmed by her song falling into gas burners turned on high.

The flame on a stove was never the same. It had a bad hangover,
didn't remember the many matches lit when its starter broke down.

My grandmother rolled paper into a funnel,
stole fire from the pilot to light the stubborn burner on the right.
Crimson burned blue on the white paper, its folded edges
curled black like lace ruffle on a skirt.

The finicky flame can't comment on its magic.
The thousands of tortillas and pancakes cooked over the years.
How I burned myself roasting a hot dog campfire style.
How a melted pencil smudged under my sister's eyelid makes her beautiful.

My grandmother noticed the time, almost noon.
She needed to make three dozen tortillas to feed her family of thirteen.
The show over, she blew the match into a swirl of gray squiggles,
snuffed before it had a chance to burn hot on her finger.

Funny, how fire is a story, waiting.

Boyhood Bop: B Train

The story is simple

A bored boy playing by
the railroad tracks
doing what inner city boys do best
drive their mothers batty
hang by the railroad

sin sifts softly
chug-a-chug-a-choochoo-chug-a-chug-a-choo

Manny found a black man's toes
by the railroad
he dumped his marbles out of his treasured jar
and tucked the toes away
Bury these toes, he thought but couldn't resist
telling Tony and Oscar, scaring his sister Blanca
who ran to mama who said it was a sin to keep
a man's body parts

sin sifts softly
chug-a-chug-a-choochoo-chug-a-chug-a-choo

A boy too curious boxed in the ears
mama's regret, the paddle wins again
He never picked up a spray can to tag a wall
Can't say the same
for Oscar, Tony, or the rest
A Black man's toes a blessing taught Manny a lesson

sin sifts softly
chug-a-chug-a-choochoo-chug-a-chug-a-choo

Porch Days

I'm six and I sit on the porch Indian style.
My best friend Aurora makes the number four with her legs.
We sit and listen to the slapping sound our thighs make against red concrete.

Aurora lives next door. She says she's from
El Salvador, the tiniest country in the world.

We stop our flopping to compare skin color.
Aurora's skin is lighter, a hint of burnt vanilla.
Melinda, you're dark! Aurora loves to say.

It's true. I am so brown, Aurora chants
so, so, suck my toe, all the way to Mexico.

After Aurora moved away, I forgot about being darker.
I stopped listening to my thighs. But I still hear
Aurora's voice when I think of summer.

Ramona Street

Remember the short time you lived with both parents in a one-bedroom
apartment on Ramona Street. The 710 sounds like a river outside your
window. Make believe the freeway is the Mississippi because you know
how to spell the word.

Hug your rabbit with the ear singed by a light bulb.
Cradle her. Ignore the burnt smell and loose button eye.
The eye on your mother's swollen face is worse.

See your childhood room. Lift the lacquered top of your mother's music box.
Love Story plays on repeat until you break the brass knob.
Take the box apart. Put it back together again.
Continue to fix broken things.

El South-Central Cucuy

My uncle said I wouldn't have a life.
Sorry, la little Minnie, he snarked,
Dah, ha, ha, he laughed.
If the Cucuy doesn't get you, the Bomb will.

South Central L.A. sounds like a battlefield with its random bullets,
helicopter searches for who knows whose father, brother, son,
enemies of the state, the police call them.

The Bomb will end everything, but el Cucuy
is scarier than any bomb or bullet
flying through my window at night.

Stray bullets like sonic popcorn punctured our television in the living room.
Crackles and pop-pop sounds force me to hit the ground.

Sneaky tires of a car turning too slowly force me to roll off my warm bed.
Welcome to my barrio.

Bullets spared me, but took the young lives of three on our street.
Bullets and bombs are visible, unlike el Cucuy.

You can't see the Cucuy who lurks in the hallway, under the bed and in the closet.
The boogeyman with devil's feet waits to touch your hair in the dark,
in a crowded house on Albany Street in South Central L.A.

Sudden Stranger

You appeared behind a trashcan,
an unkempt man with long teeth and fingers,
like the Big Bad Wolf wanting
to eat Little Red Riding Hood.

You weren't a cute and fuzzy man of trash,
like the Muppet named Oscar,
grouchy and green, living in a can.

You weren't helpful on rainy days,
like mom's garbage man, taking the trash,
the recycling too, telling her
it's okay to go back inside.

When you sneered at my piece of pizza and
all you wanted was one measly bite,
I ran away from your tall shadow,
oblivious of your words.

Bozo Takes a Hit for Dad

The bouncy plastic creature stood taller than my shadow.

My small hands didn't know how to accept the gift from my father,

the horrendous surrogate with perpetual and painful smile,

surprised eyebrows, swollen tomato nose, and fiery sideways horns for hair.

He told me to pretend Bozo was him,

said I could yell at it, punch it to exhaustion,

lecture it when he didn't do right by me.

Silence was my ungrateful answer to my father, until he got the hint and left.

With nowhere to hide the larger than life doll,

I looked to Duke; the German Shepherd always had answers.

Get him, boy. No use.

Duke darted out of the room.

The framed Guardian Angel leading two kids to safety helped.

I took the photo down, pulled out the nail,

turned Bozo around, prepared to stab him in the back.

All I had to do was pull the plug.

Bozo let out his last sigh,

settled like an evil puddle of colors at my feet.

Loyal Duke returned, then sprinted away

with Bozo in his mouth. Good boy, good dog!

Abuela's Higuera

I remember the time your father was trying to kill my daughter with a brick. Beneath the shade of my fig tree, he beat her. She stood there, letting him slap and punch her. Your abuelo told me to stay out of it. But if it weren't for me, the good-for-nothing would've killed mija with a brick. On my way out the kitchen door I grabbed my rolling pin. He didn't even see me coming when I whacked him on the head. I would've finished him off with his own brick if your mother hadn't stopped me. *You'll get in trouble with the police*, she said. The hell I cared if I got in trouble. He was on my property, trying to kill my daughter. After that happened, the sad fig tree didn't give good fruit anymore. Only these dried little nuggets with sticky milk. We had to wait a whole year for the fig to produce again. Your father ruined the tree. My poor higuera.

Dancing with Zorro's Ghost

My father is in prison.
He is dancing with Zorro's ghost and all the unwanted
Don Juans and Romeos of the world. He wears an imaginary Panama hat
to match his infectious Panamanian smile.

He stands tall in front of his bare bunk bed, wears his country
like a gold cross and yells,
I'm from Panama. His voice booms beyond iron bars.
I'm from Panama. I don't belong here.

Being an exotic man from Panama reduced his sentence
to nine years in Folsom Prison for a crime of passion and stupidity.

Too late to trump the law with angelic eyes and Panamanian pride.
Locked up for being crazy and off his meds,
wielding a sword like Zorro, drawing a gun like Zapata under a wide sombrero.
His final card not good enough to keep him home on parole.

How do I talk to the charismatic lunatic, my father,
the criminal with the psycho gene and tangled gypsy beard?

Like Don Quixote, my father fights windmills in the night.
Tricky, kinky-haired Tony slipped a piece of metal
into his sock to protect his coffee-bean colored skin.
The blow like a shooting star. He'll never know his own strength.

With his enemy tucked away for the purple night, my father wrote poetry.
His farewell letter to his daughter a fable about a turtle and a hare.
Secluded in a darker place for his sock trick, six months in the hole,
nestled like the Man in the Iron Mask, dreaming of sunshine,
sleep, papá, sleep.

Things to Carry

One key on a simple ring.

Twenty one-dollar bills for the vending machines.

A sealed package of tissues.

One comb or brush to look pretty for your prisoner.

A clear plastic baggie to hold your possessions.

Photo tokens for a family portrait in prison.

The prized photo will remind your father to be on good behavior

but you don't like the image of yourself.

Your hair's all wrong and your eyes are closed,

too many chins in the way.

You wanted to lose weight before making

the historic prison visit.

You promise to send him a better one

but his torn face, cataract blue eyes, beg you to keep

the lousy loony tune background photo.

You show him your ID just to prove

you weren't always lugging

the extra worry around your waist.

Your ID locks you in and sets you free.

You stay until the badges and gun holsters kick you out,

tell you to board the school bus back to your car.

When your father tells you how proud he is of you,

you force a smile, promise to return, stay a whole weekend,

but the last thing you want is another prison visit.

Remember Persephone

Visiting hours until 2 p.m.

My sister and I arrive at the concrete gates,

sorry we dawdled all morning

in search of breakfast, coffee, atm.

Storefronts allured us with name brand bargains.

Dad has been waiting all morning to see us.

Lost opportunities add up to an eternity.

We pass through the first gate, checkpoint number one.

Shoes off, pink jacket tossed in a gray bin,

board a sky blue bus.

Checkpoint number two,

metal door crashes to a close.

We're locked in now.

The belly of hell smells of sulfur, sweat, and betrayal.

Emily stops to use the women's bathroom.

I refuse to touch anything, especially a toilet.

Checkpoint number three, we visit our father.

Pull out our coins for a picnic from the vending machines,

Pepsi, boneless chicken wings, pecan pie.

My sister offers me her soda.

I remember Persephone's story and

refuse to eat or drink anything.

Names and Numbers

When I was three, I easily ignored you

the rare occasion you dropped by to visit.

When I was six, you wanted to be called Daddy.

Tony, I'd say.

Daddy, you'd repeat.

We dropped the game knowing six-year-old girls always win.

At twenty I formally called you by your full name, Antonio Palacio.

These were the years I easily forgot about you.

You disappeared, absorbed by new families.

I told myself I didn't care.

At thirty-eight, I visit you in prison.

You want to be called Pops,

like the cereal I never liked.

Pops as in popsicle.

Pops as in pop goes the weasel,

pop pop, bang bang goes the gun you fired six times,

the noise as you tried to shoot your child and his mother,

the bullet ricocheting off their car.

Pops, the denim-clad prisoner.

Pops, the Panamanian accent I had almost forgotten,

a new surprising softness to your voice,

the sudden lilt of palm trees and *arroz con gandules*.

Pops, a tall, bald man I do not know.

Sister's Shakedown at Steven's Steakhouse,
City of Commerce, California, 2008

My sister dances Salsa at Steven's Steakhouse.
She'll dance with any sweaty or flashy dude.
When I tell her not to talk to every man, she eyes me funny.

Sister's too young to know
how mother made her mark
as a disco Queen at Steven's Steakhouse.

Nothing changes at Steven's. Chipped disco lights swirl until closing.
Regulars hover long after
cleaning their ten dollar all-you-can-eat steak plate.

Rita, the sexiest little mama, puts her kids to bed early.
She promises herself one more night, hiked up in heels,
before shedding her dancing shoes for soccer mom sneakers.

Frog faced men, numbers one, two, and three,
belly up to cheap drinks, a slow bolero, and the chance to hold a woman tight.
Pretend the song will last forever. Never mind frogs can't dance.

Miguel from South Gate knows he's the best dancer.
He can't wait to leave the factory job he's had since high school,
kiss his mother goodbye, then hit the scene.

Everyone holds their breath for Phantom Dancer Number Nine.
He's the good dancer every girl, ages 17 to 67, wants,
lives alone, buys the lady a drink, smells clean, not too perfumy.
My sister packs her girlfriends in her Honda.
Her three friends, Rebecca, Cecilia, and Irene, don't mind
her older sister mixing with them.
Rebecca's blonde hair shimmers like neon tetras
lighting up a lonely living room.
She reels in the guys.

Irene, obedient child,
responsible at 26, designated driver,
never complains.

Cecilia shimmies to the bar. She and the telepathic waiter square away drinks,
guess correctly, hand me gin, not an electric panty remover, the latest cocktail
dangles empty promises from a plastic swizzle stick.

My sister, the tallest woman on the floor, serves up long bare legs,
grooves in stilettos, traces precise ballroom moves.
She winces at my fuchsia encased legs, steady feet, fitted in boxy ballet flats.

Nerdy glasses and bright tights separate me from the twenty-year olds.
In my day, we made up our own dance. Fuchsia was the hip color,
a holdover from Punk Rock days.

I shuffle through a clumsy cha-cha, pray for the girls
to end this evening of dance.
Two a.m., my eyes beg for sleep.

Emily gives her older sister points for staying awake.
She moves with a fire pulsing through her, a teasing invitation in her eyes,
spots Phantom Dancer Number Nine and makes her move.

But he's already pulled me close,
forced a twirl,
an easy trick with a five-foot-zero dance partner.

Phantom Dancer Number Nine chose bright pink tights over bare legs.
The girls offer me a green eye from their seats. Cecilia's shy wave
carries the unfairness of seeing an older married woman have all the fun.

Time to leave and the fire moves
to my sister's eyes, proud
her older sister closed down the place.

Día de la Independencia

las estrellas de mi país
brillan azul en su bandera rayada
blanco con rojo de sangre ajena.

el aire de mi país es dulce de leche
mezclado con sal de mar y sudor,
trabajo de gente invisible,

inmigrantes nacidos en Aztlán,
buscan allá, donde mi país
cambia nombre.

niños con lenguas moradas,
uva en sus raspados,
juegan inocentes a indios y vaqueros.

Independence Day

the stars of my country
shine blue in its striped flag
white and red with foreign blood.

the air of my country is caramel
mixed with sea salt and sweat,
work of invisible people,

immigrants born in Aztlán
search over there, where my country
changes names.

children with purple tongues,
grape in their snow cones,
innocent play of cowboys and indians.

Mala Latina

Mala Latina!
Two words take their sweet time to wash over me, sticky
like molasses, a slow brown substance insult
thrown my way from schoolyard kids and a teacher
who said I lingered over my words too long,
held up the rest for recess. Rolled syllables
in my head until I stuttered a sound, soft and shy,
an answer, at last. I think before I speak.

Fast forward to a loose gravel exchange in the parking lot
of Gold's Gym. Sunshine and sweat didn't end in waves,
smiles, and high fives from a friendly voice, my weekly
chance to practice Spanish, a rarity in the lost desert of Arizona.
An hour ago, fat and sugar duked it out on a stationary cycle.
Morning chore done. Time to enjoy.

How many children do you have?
None. No tengo.

Mala Latina!
His verbal bomb stuns me. I revert to molasses,
the world turns to slow motion and so do I.
Speechless, I fail to counter with a quick-witted roar.
My barren womb on trial. My 27-year old body recoils.
I drive away from two words. Dust on my tongue.
Mala Latina.

Notes to Self

1. You have always been lonely, but never alone.

Remember, the bigger hand holding yours?
Later, the hand is hairy and strong,
the way a lover's should be.

2. You once thought you were alone when your banshee cries
bounced off four walls.

You were told to finish, come out when you were ready to smile.
The smiling part caused a fresh fit to fume from your ears,
wail out your throat.

3. Don't sink into that dark place from which there is no return.

Romance the devil,
until your cries are a distant memory and
you're ready for church and candy.

4. Alone is drowning in the river before you are dead.

Ask yourself, do you still want that white dress?
Or would you rather sleep forever...

5. Last and most important item.

If you are still reading this, burn these words,
pretend you never wrote them.

The Calm After

Words poured out of you like a rainstorm
first a trickle, followed by a gush,
crashing louder than a hurricane,
no need to argue over walking too fast.

Words burned out of you
like wild fires jumping the 101
first a tree, followed by a roof,
our house reduced to a charred concrete slab.

You always whistled until your lips
trembled with a hum all their own.

The neighbor's sprinkler mindlessly waters the sidewalk and
only their dog hears your plea. Too bad it's been years
since a crimson crowned mockingbird
carried your song to my ears.

How sweet to sleep on your side, a cocoon of pillows.
Most nights I forget our hyphenation burned
in the fireplace you erased.

Tea Fire 2008, Santa Barbara, CA

Think anything but
burnt English Breakfast or charred Earl Grey.
The Tea Fire consumes recklessly like the drunk my father once was.

Santa Anas and sundowners force me to grab
photos, phone, laptop, and pink fuzzy slippers,
a jumble thrown into my car.

I wait for the fire to end its binge,
examine valuables, feel mocked by the shoe box of photos I saved.

A parade of people who exist only in photographs, faces
who no longer fuel lost friendship.
My father relegated to an old shoe box.

Why do I hesitate before lighting a match?

2

Air
Carries
Her

Last Generation of Tourists

Climb the tallest pyramid of Tikal. Reach
the top with cheers from Europeans who
know how scared you are. Sing a child-
hood song to help you make it back
down. *She'll be coming around the moun-
tains when she comes.* Accept small bites
from tábanos in the jungles of Petén, the
merciless flies with hard yellow shells for
wings don't care that mosquitoes have
plunged into your poisoned blood first.
In Antigua, avoid being seen as a walk-
ing wallet. You're a friend or a cousin as
long you continue to linger over jewelry
and weavings. Women and their daugh-
ters hold onto their tradition of wearing
flowered huipiles and long skirts when a
picture is worth an extra dollar in the
long bartering process. Say no to the in-
flated price, feel lousy later for pocketing
the quetzales. Sneak pictures of faces too
tired to smile. Worry you may be the last
generation of tourists to see the sight of
ancient men, dressed in colorful shirts
and pants. Dream in Spanish as volca-
noes sleep underneath moonlight on
Lago Atitlan. Be grateful for the sound of
the wind, taking flight in sacred lands.

disconcerted crow

if only his bird suit fit, he
grumbles and caws, drives
away his dove friends, he
pecks at uneven bristles, he
flaps and folds starched wings.
familiar feathers hang all wrong
like borrowed funeral clothes

far from dead, he
disrobes with a thud,
lands on my roof, he
morphs into a toddler,
crashes giant steps, he
skates swift on loose shingles
calls out to his pity of doves

when no one answers, he
takes up his post on a wire
outside my window, he
hunches his seaweed back,
beak snug in breast, and he
is an old man again

Outlaw Zone

Arizona,
lull me back
to sun rays on mountains,
full moon hikes and coyote cries,
heat from windless days, where
people dared build
cities in a desert.

Don't piss me off, Arizona.
Don't go back to those ugly years
of no Dr. King days with your
sweeps and roundups,
sounds like a rodeo, ¿que no?
Don't prey on your people, gente
browner than an Arizona sunset.

Shoes, you say.
You can tell by their shoes.
Shoes say it all:
inmigrante, illegal.

Don't tell me where you came from
or how the West was won
or why you think, Arizona,
land of little water, chollas,
bottlebrush sage, ocotillos, saguaros
is only for those whose skin burns pink.

Arizona,
Add air to your name,
Air-uh-zone-uh. Air-a-

zone for legals,
ahh-ry-zo-naaa.

Arizona,
Don't forget which country you come from.

The Framed Virgin

In a desert called México, high on a hill
She appeared to an Indian named Juan Diego.
A miracle, roses and her image on his robe.
She filled his being with prayer and satisfaction.

Five centuries later, a young man named Juan Grande found her image in a
wooden frame.
The vibrant colors reminded him of Her miracle.
He took the portrait to his young wife, Victoria, who was pregnant with his
tenth child.
Victoria prayed.

Virgencita, nine boys I have given you
to fight and defend your land. Nine boys who will leave me to raise their own
families.

Virgencita, give me a girl to take care of me in my old age.
Mamà used to say, have girls and you'll eat chicken. Have boys and you'll live
alone.
Victoria had a girl.
And the girl married a Black man.

¿Quien es ese negro?

Juan Grande's words echo in the hallway.
That's Blanca's boyfriend. Victoria's reply fills the room.
She hides her regret in begging for a girl named Blanca.
Blanca will leave with the dark Panamanian named Antonio.

Nineteen years pass before Victoria apologizes to the Virgen.
She bargains and explains.
Her prayer is answered.
Blanca gives birth to a daughter.

México Lindo

A question hangs heavy in the air like a day wasted.

A day of nothing
Ten toes wiggling in the sand and a beating heart are all she needs.

A day of nothing.
The noise of working men is too loud
for languid ears. The con artists at the beach waste their
breath. The pregnant mangy dog scavenges on three legs.

A day of nothing.
La gringa isn't bothered by the question of who she is. She needs to taste the
salty lime and sweet mango in the land of amigos and tacos.

She's dressed for quick service. Face hidden beneath her
wider than necessary hat. She looks like candy with her chocolate
silk pants, a little lace over her breasts.

"Se-ñor, por fa-vor, a pack of cigarettes," her crooked
voice screams. She wants another Corona too.
No time to wait for the change. "Keep it."

She has some extra pe-sos. She didn't fall for the coffee-
eyed child begging her to buy the silver bracelet.
No, gra-ci-as. She knows a good bargain.

Don't walk, strut, you're fabulous!
She tosses her sassy hair back,
shakes out her towel.

Before relaxing, she dips a toe in the pool.
Paradise.

She wiggles,
settles in for sun,
shoves aside the warm bottle, grabs a cold one,
salutes to no one and the world.

It's 3 p.m. on Tuesday in ma-ña-na time,
her day of nothing.
Did she pack
her
pink
pumps?

The Blue House

Que Pinche Luck, Frida.
Frida whose face I know better than my own.
Stoic and strong
a single eyebrow stretched in solidarity,
a hint of a mustache makes you more beautiful.
¿y porque no?

Pain immortalized, pain perfected.
a derailment of bones, a dead foot, a dead child.
Yet beautiful you stand, bella Frida.

One day I'll tell you my story of a raw elbow, a fractured ankle bone, a dead
mother.

Yours is a kaleidoscope
crying louder than La Llorona.
Suffering splashed on canvas,
as strong as red,
as gnarled as yellow,
as dismembered as fuchsia,
as lonely as the cobalt of your house, the heart of Coyoacán,
the place of where there is praise of coyotes,
Coyoacán, the place where Frida Kahlo was born,
Coyoacán, the place where the blue house resides.

Icon of self-love
Coyoacán is yours.
Frida, can you imagine how the world beyond Aztlán admires your pain?

Chinaberry Tree on Calle de Parian, Mesilla, New Mexico

Painted leaves of yellow. Wasn't the Chinaberry green
a week ago? Green, like a pistachio paleta,
ready to drip down my hand.

It looks as though paint has splashed her left side lemon.
Her yellowed branches a reminder of yesterday's
miracle of too many catfish in the arroyo.

Like the tree's leaves, I long to shake out my feathers,
grow skyward and take flight
beneath the corn blue sky.

Mesilla Sunset

A cold wind floats briskly from the Organ Mountains,
echoing a chorus of voices, desperate to be singled out like La Llorona,
wading in the Río Grande, forever.

I shiver when I think I hear laughter of a mother and daughter,
the rustling of twigs from a nearby park, and then
silence. The river doesn't care who joins her.

A white wisp from a thunderhead cloud and only the pecan orchards
enjoy drowning in a sweet flood.

On the plaza, a parade of colors stroll by San Albino's Church.
Your footsteps rattle like red chile seeds, dried
until you've memorized the scent of New Mexico.

Ancient cries for a history grander than a mosaic marker are muffled
by noise over the Gadsden Purchase and Billy the Kid.

The turquoise sky so vast, you'll never see the same cloud twice.
Was it the coconut cloud, twisted like a bear?

Or was it you, shape shifting, becoming a cicada,
buzzing in praise of Saturday's pink twilight, a Mesilla sunset.

Balloon Fiesta

Four men run, chase clouds of their breath.
A misshapen ball tumbles free like a child.
Reds and oranges shoot past neighbor portals.

Bob grabs thick ropes,
a chance to help a stranger, save the day,
fetch the world in his hands, tame
the balloon like a bear roped down to its last breath
until silk falls over.

Lucky he wore his shearing gloves.
No one from Corrales or Albuquerque
built the wayward balloon with slippery knots
for hand holds. The team in matching shirts and
familiar logo hug and high-five.

Bob retreats to the adobe on his grandmother's land,
heats his coffee in the microwave, sits
and waits for the next glint of shooting silk.

Sin Vergüenza Swagger

My sister drinks in Panamá, rubs
cinnamon colored sand on her cheeks,
dabs more mud on her face and we
walk deeper into the jungle.

Oblivious to venomous snakes, our chanclas
sink brown feet into pretty clay. We pull each other up,
lose ourselves in song and the wild. City girls free.

When a Ngöbe-Buglé, carrying a machete finds us, he asks
why my sister wears war paint. She is always ready
for battle, draws her rules in lipstick.

The answer to all questions lead to our isthmus hips,
our father's sin vergüenza swagger.
We find pride in hips and lips everywhere.

Little girls wear their sisters' tight blouses.
Grandmas and mamas serve up sensuality sweeter
than any ripe fruit, says the song blasting from every bus.

On our last day in Panamá, the taxi driver wants to take
my sister home, but remembers his hair-raising wife.
Sin vergüenza swagger. He reminds us the conquistadors
staged the conquest of all the Americas from Panamá.

Panamá, curvy isthmus, dizzying land bridge, turn
too fast and you'll lose North. North is irrelevant
when you consider a city sacked and burned,
when a country sells out its own people for foreign dollars.

It took a trip to Panamá to understand my father's sin vergüenza swagger,
sprung from volcan Baru, blessed by two oceans, bathed in sweat.
May he remember the smell of coconuts and sea salt from his prison cell.

Grasshopper in the Box

A grasshopper jumped out her U-haul box.
The cri-cri-tinkle-tinkle sound wasn't a
a broken dish. She sighed happy,
made a grasshopper's day.

Donna doesn't know how
faded green wings, gone
out the window, means luck
stronger than a voodoo charm.

A sticky day in Bayou St. John,
nature gone to traffic, grasshopper
gone to stray cat, stray cat gone. Count
your blessings, her mother once whispered.

On one rare occasion, Mamma
remembered her third child.
Hard to keep up with all six.
She stirred her whiskey sour.

Diana, Daisy, Donna, Duane, Deborah, Margaret.
Margaret, her mother's name, too hard to think
of another name in major D.
Duck, duck, duckies.

One duck lives in a tree house.
She opened a box and
let out a loud grasshopper
as annoyed as her neglected city.

Quince Jam

Roberto knows the tricky fruit is best
used in jam. He doesn't listen to
culinary norms, but tries it
in a port sauce on a rack of lamb.

The fruit looks like a lemon gone wrong,
wanting
to be a sweet pear.

Its name squeezes member and embryo:
membrillo.
Not too pretty to a foreign ear,
but music to my native tongue.

I stick my finger into sweet paste,
taste brilliance paired with manchego cheese.

An ounce of quince and a second
of sweetness to forgive
the sorrows of a lost home.

The Angel in the House

She slips a fairy's dress over her head. The fragile
armor clings lovingly to her sides. A disguise she's
worn so well she no longer remembers the day she
snagged it from Filenes's Basement. She slides into
her second-hand glass slippers. Translucent wedges
fit so well, she's suddenly tall enough to propel a
star back to its attic of dust and dirt. She releases
more frantic butterflies scurrying scared from her
belly. A glimpse of colorless moon reflects the shy
person of her youth. She smiles at the woman who
refused to be the angel chained in the house, a
proud owner of a solar-powered gossamer dress,
domestic wings not included.

The Old Mission's Bell

Me llamo Santa Barbara.
I am a discarded bell,
too old to ring the days away.
I carry my city's name.
Me llamo Santa Barbara.

Santa Barbara, discarded bell.
Santa Barbara, dethroned saint, calendars say.
Santa Barbara, city of the Old Mission,
Santa Barbara, twin bell towers, red.

Red to mimic near mountains and sky,
setting in sun-shimmering gloria.

From my round capped home, see
the ocean, a holy shade of blue, beyond
San Nicolas, once home to another
lost woman, christened Juana Maria.

Saint Barbara, imprisoned in a single
tower with a trinity of windows,
discarded, discalced, but revered.

Your bare feet never walked
on smooth adobe floors. Your
robes never soaked in spouting
water from a bear totem, our
Chumash lavanderia.

No worries for red skies or red roses.
Your name remains.
This old Mission holds your head true,
namesake of sword and palm.
Me llamo Santa Barbara.

How to Make a Mediocre Poem Sing

1. Vary your cadence. Pair a primeval word with a root like parsnip or potato.

2. Enunciate. Pretend each meter was your very last breath.

3. Ask an age old question. Why is a raven like a writing desk?

4. Say teacup, add another P word and a penitent tilt to your head.

5. Throw in Shakespearean characters, Cordelia, Portia, Prospero.
Pretend you were the Bard himself, making up the names for the first time.

6. Wear a long white buttoned down shirt. Leave some of the buttons undone.
Make sure your pants and fingers have ink stains.

7. Before lifting the bangs from your eyes, again, take a slow sip from your water
bottle, careful to unscrew the top slowly.

8. For an extra memorable performance, entertain them with more than poetry.
Sing a song in a foreign language, *quand il me prend dans ses bras.*

9. Memorize a line or two, look into the audience's eyes. Smile.

10. Talk birds, beaks, and plumes (P word, again). When your audience of poets
coos and awes, you've done it. Take a bow.

Chasing Self: Yinka Shonibare & a Flying Machine for Every Man, Woman, and Child

Santa Barbara Museum of Art, April 2009

A frock of green and every color in between for a spin in her flying machine.

—the present—

She writes a letter to her future self.
Leaps into kaleidoscope flight. Loses self in Damask space.
Her head precedes her.
No choice but to stare square into her past.

—the future—

Her former self hovers over green horizon.
Hands remain strong.
Waist painfully thin, as always.
Dress morphs from fish to triangles,

fabric hiked up avoids a colorful crash
wonder bustle wrinkles rich brocade
until forced to teeter sideways, straddle a wrong country,
France, in just the right outfit.

Can't be seen in anything but her finest
or those who own the strange land will
know she does not belong.
Silly to think things would be different in the future.

She no longer tries to remember the name her mother gave her.
Green, red, purple, blue propellers accelerate her progress.
Mother of two head-weak children. Her husband, in the lead,
has lost his head too. Onward, heads roll to France's past.

Pedaling backwards her childhood is no longer a fun place to visit.
But the longing stitches an itch in her boots.
She suddenly knows how the past is like the favorite outfit,
tossed out years ago, her soul yearns to wear.

—the past—

She was the perfect child.
Her mother dressed her in boys' clothing.
Not always Mrs. Blank,
but a question mark, a riddle her mother solved.

—somewhere in time—

Her flying machine whisks her to perfection,
beyond monsters disguised in beautiful gowns,
beyond slaves,
beyond fanciful backstabbers
who dream without reason.

Panamanian Percentage

His heart thumps Panama, where he's from.
His hair curls Jamaica, where his mother was born.
His arms smash Colombia, where his absent father called home.
His sides laugh East India and England, where his grandparents met.
His rhythm taps Africa, where his great grandmother lived and died.

I own his crooked smile, a slight curl
of the upper lip. My teeth straightened
by braces. He said he footed the bill,
but he never paid for jack.

Some call my sister a dreamsicle.
She stands a whole foot over me.
Her ballsy stride, the stretch of confidence
our father used when he thought
he'd never get caught.

Impossible to tell where I begin
or end, where our
Panamanian percentage meets.

The half made whole by my mother's feet,
my feet. Feet furious enough to power a car,
squat Indian feet showing off red toes
in an even row, overshadowed by
an upturned big toe, hitching a ride to Mexico,
where the Rio Bravo roars.

Water

3 Water Rises South

Laughter

The story of my mother touches the wind and rattles me off
balance, raises the small hairs on my forearms, my skin no
longer feels my own. I long to be cradled by a cloud, sus-
pended and sheltered. I listen to the words of the Grand-
mother Spirit. My elder says look beneath your skin and
you'll see the loneliness in your veins. I hear drumming, a
familiar wail of pain. The drums stop. The story of my
mother is as ordinary as once upon a time there was a
happy woman who lived a short life before dying, leaving
behind a daughter. The pages between the beginning and
the end are filled with laugher. A girl with wild hair the
color of the Río Grande sinks her feet into the muddy river
and says, you laugh like my grandmother. I laugh harder
because the wild woman is my mother.

Distant Suds

Bubbles, filled with his ugly words pop, burst,
evaporate. "No, tú no sabes."
Distant suds are all he has left.

She tells the lonely grandfather she can wash a dish.
She's seen the TV ladies do it, she's seen him do it
a million times.

What's that your soaking in?
It's Palmolive,
much better than Dove, the TV voice says.

The girl with messy long hair drags a chair to the sink.
He turns on the water for her. It burns her hands.
She forgot to ask for the yellow gloves the TV ladies wear.

His soft, translucent skin numb, burned so badly
he can no longer feel the scalding water.
He don't need no yellow gloves.

"You don't know how.
You're a trouble-making-think-you-know-it-all-little girl.
You'll never marry."

He takes pity on her, rubs butter on her burnt fingers.
I bet you didn't know that butter is good for burns,
Little-miss-I-can-read-n-speak-n-English.

She knows his heart is more scorched than her small hand.
Strike, light, blow gray curls between words and untold dreams.
The old man dreams of being a boy again.

He remembers a time when his mamá ironed his calzones
in the morning and then ironed his tortillas in the afternoon,
made the tortilla evenly brown, perfect just for him.

Those were the good ol' days.
His wife never uses a cast iron to smooth out his chones or his tortillas.
She's too busy watching her novela.
And his sons, his granddaughter? They can't wash a dish.

He pauses for a small smile, thinks about the house he left behind to cross
the border, pick peaches and, finally,
become an American dish washer on disability.

En los Esteikes Senaikes

En los Esteikes Senaikes barren dinero, Tía.
              Mijo, no barren nada.
O, sí tía!
ya me voy a los Esteikes Senaikes.
Me pongo mis Levis y le doy un abrazote
a Mickey Mouse.
Tía, ven conmigo.
Bautízate en el Río Bravo
Nos vamos a hacer millonarios, Tía
En los Esteikes Senaikes.

In the United Steaks

In the United Steaks, people sweep money off the streets.
> Sweetheart, don't be silly, they don't even sweep up dust.

O, yes, Auntie!
I'm going to the United Steaks.
I'll wear my Levis and give a big ole kiss
to Mickey Mouse.
Come with me, Auntie.
Baptize yourself in the Río Bravo.
We're gonna be millionaires, Auntie, over there,
in the United Steaks.

Life Beyond the Río Grande

Swim with your clothes held high above the water,
cross to the other side.

Follow the train tracks to the Concrete River,
fall flat on its glittered bank.

Don't mind the blood trickling from your mouth or the loose tooth;
you'll fix it, house your very own Hollywood smile.

Turn left towards the Sierra Madres. Take a deep breath before you run naked
through the Glendale Galleria. Wake up from your dream, again.

Say goodbye to huaraches and pulque,
forever. Don't fool yourself. You won't go back.

Keep your red cowboy boots, your tattoo of the Virgen de Guadalupe,
    your mother's huipil.
When did you become so afraid of being alone?

Wear an American flag t-shirt over your push-up bra, sing the American song,
hear the bullet snap. You're in America, now.

Arroyo Burro Beach

A beach in Santa Barbara faces South.

Sand falls between open fingers.

Copper eyes reflect my caramel face as

sea water blesses a black dog's tail.

Broken shells and tangled red kelp crunch.

Under my numb feet, sun sets on iridescent bubbles

hovering over tar stained pebbles. In the distance

oil rigs look like battle ships poised to defend

a new way of Chumash life. Ocean and mountains

hide our red roof tiled city. Above, a white pelican

steals blue fish, belts out a triumphant squeal.

Below, translucent sand crabs jump joyously,

as if in church shouting hallelujah. I pause

to taste salt air and receive a shy gift

of a kiss against the mango colored sky.

Waves crashing so hard

sound drowns out reason.

Be Bop for Blanca

Her name's irrelevant if all you see is a color.
Her name is foolish if all you see is a brown girl named Blanca
Hitchhiking to New Orleans, falling in love with a Black man,
a scandal smaller than a lunar footprint.
Make no mistake, colorblind is her answer.

Falling in love during the Summer of Sixty-Nine.
Ideas sold down the river.

History repeats like a riled raven screeching.
Henrietta hitched a ride to a Quadroon Ball.
Henrietta loved to dance. She'll dance and sway,
sway and dance. Won't let no paper bag test
get in her way. History repeats.
If the darker gal is prettiest, let her in. If the girl
can dance, let her in. History repeats.

Falling in love during the Summer of Sixty-Nine.
Ideas sold down the river.

Blanca knows the rules.
This ain't no Quadroon Ball in New Orleans.
We're talking about a Sock Hop Prom in East L.A.
and he's not welcome.
Let the young people dance, dance, dance.
Let the young people bop, bop, bop.

Falling in love during the Summer of Sixty-Nine.
Ideas sold down the river.

He's duded out in buttercream leather,
'fro fanning across America,
declaring his love atop platform shoes.

He spoke her language, Spanish, and said he was from Panamá,
this man who everyone called Black, forbidden
to a colorblind girl named Blanca.

She, in her Pocahontas glamour, tasseled suede dress, go-go boots,
fits squarely snug beneath his arm, belonging
before there were lost flowers to sing about.

Falling in love during the Summer of Sixty-Nine.
Ideas sold down the river.

False River, New Roads, Louisiana

Dip your feet into False River.
A man catches catfish.
His success reveals gold
in his teeth. He tells you
he plans on taking you home.
Guess what's for dinner, Darlin'?

Your nervous laughter imitates
the Mardi Gras Queen you forgot about,
the one who complimented you on your skin.
What a healthy glow, golden bronze!
She avoided the fisherman's question,
asked only with his russet eyes:
Are you black, brown, Creole, or what?

You smile like a river, false
as a faint hug or a lake, curved
into a cut-off grin, sporting perfect
postcard alligator teeth.

Your feet make daisies in the water.
Wind rustles sugar cane and
centuries of sweet old secrets
spare your unworked hands.

Water Mark

A river runs beneath my house
white foam, greenblue mud, a Eureka stream of gold.
Water so urgent, rushing like a stampede, catching
tomorrow's California claim jumpers.

Wild west talk of black bears and banana bread.
Don't leave your doggy biscuits in the car.

The river rattles innocence and much to my surprise my heart aches
for the child I once was, before broken levees and the
floodgates of hell descending upon my town. Water rising

trumpeting untoward Mississippi
seeping into the space of sighs
pray for a rooftop rescue.

In my borrowed house in Truckee, a scene so serene
broken by the rolling river below. Woken up
by a sleepless river wailing a lullaby.
When sleep finds a crook in the neck of dreams,

I hear water, bathtub water.
Water poured into a porcelain tub,
to bathe we girls. A game invented by grownups
for three bored girls in a tub.

A sweet olive tree on Tchoupitoulas Street
scrapes against the bathroom window.

Two sisters plus the neighbor girl me all in the same tub,
naked. Sneaking peeks at what the other sister doesn't have.

Breasts, beauty marks, underarm hair, a head of wet hair, theirs
short and curly, mine long strands straining to a half-hearted twist.

Our little girl dirt leaves a water mark on the tub.
Bath salts and bubbles drain slowly.
Bless my beauty mark, one sister offers and I
receive her little girl kiss in a bathtub on Tchoupitoulas Street.

Apology to a New Orleans Tree

The water oak in front of my shotgun house
was as ordinary as beignets with café au lait.

Now, only powdered sugar clings to the table and I
am as puzzled as the squirrel flying towards a missing branch.

The oak's thick, fallen trunk hollow for some time,
long before the wind toppled the tree.

Wings flutter in dizzying fits as a mockingbird's perch
no longer points skyward, the bird

twitters towards the trunk's maze of roots,
unearthing a curbside feast of insects and worms.

The City of Jazz removes the tree limb by limb,
without giving the oak a second-line dance.

No Amazing Grace, no funeral for a tree,
no blue notes wailing towards the river.

Drown all rules. For in a game of rock, scissors, paper,
wind wins.

Who Will Pick His Apples

Joann wants a job, but not that one.
The woman with cracked nail polish,
jacket ironed smooth, blue pumps,
auburn-gray locks, waits.
Her face looks like an apple,
pinched Fuji from Washington,
displaced to Louisiana, jobless
at a Lafayette temp agency.
She can type, public schooling taught her
how to make her fingers fly.
She files, pulls answers from air.
She swallows her doily pride,
fills out forms for welfare, food stamps,
a job. Any job, but not the apple orchard job,
fifteen dollars a barrel, less than minimum
wage for her calloused, arthritic hands.

Rigoberta wants work, anything to survive.
She doesn't think of her mother, her
only sister, her nephews, her tía,
frail elders left behind, or her favorite
volcanic views of Lago Atitlán.
Wide girth, long skirt aside, she moves
short legs with pyramid climbing speed.
She picks apples two at a time.
A subtle trick with hands smaller than one
Red Delicious, crimson sweetness in her palm,
whiffs of crushed cider soak her bandana and blouse.
When INS force her to board a white van South,
she returns to Louisiana.
Boss says she's the best.
He'll take her any day
over anyone with papers.

New Orleans Native Son

An invitation to swim
one sultry August afternoon.
Water cools the scorching
day. Remaining ice clinks
in my plastic glass. The
lone rat rustling in
the banana tree won't
bother me. Crows wait
for my sweet slumber, dive-
bomb the neighbor's yard.
There is one creature
I can't ignore.
His primordial wings
spread colossal and proud.
He looks bigger poolside
as feelers twitch, sense a party.
I command him to fall
in and drown.
Nya, nya, nya
says the New Orleans
native son. So brave
he waltzes, clicks beneath
the cockroach crossing sign.
No squashing allowed.

Emerald Piles

The fig beetle's
leathery shell caught
my eye. An insect so
perfect in design,
more lustrous than
an emerald strand of
St. Patrick's Day
Mardi Gras beads.
I pick up the petrified carcass,
my first collection of dead bugs.
After Katrina, trash piles
on street corners, along
with putrid refrigerators,
wandering pets, forgotten
people, and everything
stacked high, neglected.
I wonder...
if the spills and spoils
of Mardi Gras could be
cleaned up in hours, streets
ready for the next day's parade,
why was an entire city bereft
of brilliance, left for another day,
unclaimed, no one in charge,
until politicians felt the tug of home,
saw over emerald piles
of trash, and finally heard
the noise of New Orleans,
a city demanding dignity.

Offering to Saint Roch

Water rises. Rises over rooftops,
cars, schools, neighborhoods.
A town rebuilds. You're still a wreck.

Saint Roch cures all. In gratitude, leave
your plastered body part. But you want to offer
your whole body, not just a finger or a toe.

You pray to Saint Roch, ask for his help.
Receive a divine answer. Floating is
better than drinking in the morning.

When your FEMA money arrives, you ignore
your weathered house. You build a swimming pool
instead, as if floating will save you from another
hurricane.

Four Years After Katrina

Four years after Katrina.
Time to wake up, quit smoking.
The beer, once more potable than water,
was easy. Quit carbs, no problem.
All manageable until the unnamable
becomes her sister's cancer.
Smoking returns like a found treasure in the gutter.
No longer able to fly away, she adds
layers to her being. New titanium knees
slow her sensual gait.
Only her fingers remain the same,
hand held high on bent elbow,
mannerly in the air, as if the tip
of burning paper might right misery.
At night, she sleepwalks and sleep smokes,
just a puff to finish off the good dream
where she runs on Kure beach,
tastes ocean air and saltwater caramels.
After her shower, her brief struggle with stringy hair,
she lights one for the causeway commute.
Three cigarettes carry her from New Orleans
to Mandeville. A car stalled in the fast lane means
she'll be late. She'll sweet talk the boss.
Her hybrid Creole accent betrays
practiced perfection, an actor's trick.
Her cloud seals her performance.
She prays for more sleep.

The Fisherman and the Evening News

His mind freezes. He mumbles
something about our old argument
over Barataria Bay and boat repairs.
I tell him to turn the damn thing off.

Oil sheen glosses over his eyes.
He says the sour bile in his stomach refuses to gush.
Brief flit of speech and his muscles go slack.
When his gaze fails to reflect me,
his wall stands complete.

We hear about the whales and dolphins.
Crude shining like a crow's wing,
tar washed up like poisoned licorice,
plumes of false gold drown brown pelicans.

A child's careful drawing
of oil-stained earth shakes him.
He gathers nets at his feet,
returns to mindless mending.

Before I change the channel, a sign flashes:
No More Oysters in Orleans Parish.

Earth

4 Earth Spins

Choosing a Coffin

We arrive at the cemetery you can see from the freeway. Rolling, green hills, naked statues that make Ama laugh and blush. Walk into a white office. Meet the nice white lady with the white jacket. Sit in her white chairs, stare at the pictures on the white walls. We are here to choose a coffin. I am her mother. I am her daughter. I am her brother. I am her uncle. I am her friend. Our voices fill in blank spaces. I see a plain pine box. *That one,* I say, because it's simple, like the coffin chosen for Cesar Chavez, a man my mother admired tirelessly. No grapes, I remember. *Don't be cheap, Melinda,* my uncle says. *Don't worry about the money,* my mother's friend says. My grandmother decides on the white coffin that looks like a Cadillac with pink roses on each corner, lined in pink satin for a luxurious sleep. *I knew you'd pick that one,* says the nice lady with perfect plastic Pompadour hair like Elvis. *It's our finest* she says, taking in the shades of bewildered brown faces.

A Woman Who Deserves a Good Party

A woman who deserves a good party
writes notes to her daughter,
says what needs to be said.

Give Raymond eighty dollars.
Put some lipstick on, you look awful.
It's nice to see everyone.

Her last farewell around a steel bed,
her birth to the other side.

Her closed eyes cry, squint at a painful white light.
I fail to follow her.

I hear music, the sound of heavenly harps.
Corny cherubs laugh and hold their baby feet. Until I
stop biting my numb tongue, taste my own blood,
hit the earth with a thud.

Wooden Crosses

In the cemetery where my grandmother's children are buried there are no
marbled mausoleums, no tomb stones that tell who died where or when.

A wooden cross marks the spot, no fancier than last week's faded yard sale sign.
Flowers one day, overgrown grass the next.

Only abuelita knows where to look for her babes.
She prays a rosary at home, works her beads.

She is hungry for everything she has lost. Her parents, her house, the chance
to learn beyond the third grade, her two children, Alma Rosa and Roberto.

Her whispered work on smooth blue beads makes her wonder
if her prayers are heard.

Abuela's Candle For Saint Jude

When I get some centavos together, I'm going to buy a vela para San Judas. Talk about lost causes! The collectors keep calling about your grandfather's debts, especially about that mentado Buick. Why would someone sell a car to an old man who can barely see and hasn't a dime to spare? The car dealer invited your grandfather to a fiesta to show off their new cars. Your abuelo asked me if I wanted to go. Adió, I said, who cares! They don't want your shriveled-up self to attend. Pero no, he didn't listen. Instead he put on his good trousers, los pantalones you sent him for Christmas. He never wears anything new, saves everything for a special occasion. He arrived at the dealership, saw the balloons, cookies, and music, and drove home in a brand new car, instead of taking the bus.

¡Ay que estúpida! What m'hija? No, I'm not talking about you! I'm talking to the dumb woman dressed like a huila on TV. Her short skirt showing all her nauhas. You always call when I'm watching my novela. Not all of us have a break for lonche every day. I have to watch my shows before starting dinner for Ramón. No doubt his mujer will want to come and eat too. Cállate, Dino! Ay, m'ija, did I hurt your ears? Sorry. Estos perros bark like mad every time the mailman comes, even though he always drops nothing but bills every day at the same hour, they still go crazy. They have to get their exercise by running around the house because I can't walk no more with this swollen foot, hinchado y pesado, like the rest of my body. I wish I could get rid of this girth, but I can barely walk with my bastón. I hardly eat and I still keep all this weight on. You're lucky you've always been flaquita and can afford to go buy those expensive blueberries and almendras that you like. Are you still there? You got so quiet. I thought I was talking to myself. I'm sure glad you called and not the man from the dealership.

Several months have passed since he got serious about asking for the car payment. I told him to send someone to pick up the car. Someone from the dealership came, but the car was old and damaged, not the same new car from four years ago. No pues, with all the trips across the border to visit your tía Blanca in Acuña, all the rides for my sister's kids, all the mandados and piling the cousins to go to la presa, the taking of the dogs to the vet and the yearly trip to the park for the blessing of the animals. ¡U que la! The car was no longer new and the dealership didn't want it back. Instead, the man kept calling for payments, months after we buried your abuelo.

I prayed to San Judas, asked him for the strength to make your abuelo's debts go away. I finally told the man, if you want your money, you'll have to go the cemetery, near the curb, look for my esposo's military plaque, dig up his grave, prop him up, and ask Juan Grande to pay you directly. I didn't sign anything and don't even know how to drive because my husband never allowed me to learn English, never wanted me to go to school, so forget about learning how to drive. Pues ni modo. The man said he couldn't dig him up or any of what I proposed; he even apologized for bothering me. Your grandfather's car remains on blocks in the driveway. The viejo finally stopped calling, and that's why I need to buy a candle for San Judas.

Broken Hallelujah

Lulu's aging mother lives.
Against all odds, she lives.
With disease in her bones, she lives.
Teeth gone, eyesight gone, tumor-riddled middle.
Her organs no longer function, yet she lives.

After 12 children, 21 grandchildren, 30 years of restaurant work,
70 years of marriage. She lives.

Death come take me away,
Estoy toda jodida, she groans.
Die already, her children respond.
It looks as though she finally will.

Her daughter plans her funeral,
rallies the family, every one assembled,
even Luis and the boys who crawled
under the fence of the US of A.

Funeral hymns selected and rehearsed,
necklaces to wear mamá's ashes.
Never forget the memory of the soft faced woman,
her once oxen body, smelling of comino and lavender.

Wear her dichos close to your heart.
Remember her favorite sayings?

Don't let anyone sweep your feet, a strange man will carry you away.
Don't eat while standing up, the food will settle in your legs.
Death never takes anything with him, but everything disappears little by little.
She is nothing and the whole enchilada. Until
the Virgen de Guadualupe sends her back.

She makes a full recovery.
Her organs start pumping.
Her hair grows in curly.
Lulu's aging mother lives.

When people hear the news, they laugh.
Laugh at the daughter and her
band of scattered brothers. Laugh.
Laugh with the universe.

How Else?

Her stories were ancient ones.
How could they be part of the real world?

What kind of neighbors turn into harpies,
gossip on rooftops, their bird wings betraying human faces?

What kind of girl gives birth to a disappearing pig,
only to have the agonizing event occur again and again?

What kind of mind can move boulders? *Oh, that's how
the pyramids at Tenochtitlan were built,* my grandmother said.

How else?

I didn't believe her stories because I could lie too.
Tell a fiction to get out of trouble,
write a poem to see her smile.

Who wrote this? She'd ask, knowing the childish scrawl
didn't belong to the ghost
who touched my pregnant mother's feet.

Etts and Josefina, Sisters on Montezuma Avenue

Grandma Etts and her sister Josefina shared a bed in old age,

long after each married and made her mistakes.

Two sisters wove parts to the same Afghan.

Grandma's yarn blue diamonds. Josefina's stitch purple roses.

Two sisters fried plantains for arroz con pollo,

kept the bedroom closet filled with boxes of candy for callers.

Two sisters buried one daughter-in-law named Blanca.

She loved me the best, each said.

Two sisters separated when one died in her sleep.

A stroke, stronger than a Panamanian hurricane, clouded a sister's memory.

You're Blanca's daughter, said Josefina, the sister left behind,

no recollection of the hospital room and new faces.

To Josefina, the food tastes wrong. Her life lies crooked

like the crocheted flowers that no longer make a warm shawl.

Knotted yarn pieces remain raveled, untouched by wrinkled hands.

Pictures in her brain refuse to form words.

Questions for Dad

1. Why did you have a picture of Zapata in your living room?

2. Was Zapata really my uncle?

3. When did you learn how to shoot a gun?

4. What did you do with all the coins in my Abraham Lincoln piggy bank?

5. Have you always had an interest in vocabulary and not books?

6. Do you really think you've loved all three of your wives?

7. Why didn't you introduce me to your other children earlier?

8. Besides the meds making you giddy, have you changed?

9. Why are you such a ham?

10. What do you most admire about yourself?

11. Why are you in prison?

12. Did you really think you'd get away with everything?

Blue Bop For Montezuma

My birthday gift barked back love.
Love for eating my expensive shoes, leather couch, and favorite reading chair.
This mutt's taste lacked finesse. A petulant love for pleather and plastics
didn't elude him. Handbags, raincoats, the backyard's sprinkler system
dug up like a poor man's graveyard.
The devil graced me with evil.

When I get to heaven, first thing I'll do
I'll blow my horn and call for blue

I didn't see god's face staring back at me until a woman at Petco stopped us.
Oh, the face of love, she cooed, blessing my beagle crossed lab,
casting the devil from his bugled howl. My adopted ball of
feed me, walk me, play with me, lets run together out the door around the park,
do it again before I get my cookie, please, please, now, and I'll reward you
with a canine cuddle, a sloppy kiss you can't miss, a muddied paw on your jaw,
bursts of puppy tornado through the house,
blossomed celestial blue.

When I get to heaven, first thing I'll do
I'll blow my horn and call for blue

Trick of all tricks. After our learned groove
a whole year to settle his puppy alpha dog riddle.
No silly clothes, no scraps from the table, walks when I say.
Nine years later, my loyal bundle of black fur, four white toes gifted me with a
lunar mission's vet bill.
This creature's face of love undone by a heart too large.
His spark ceased too soon. My dog dead at my feet while I was on the toilet.

When I get to heaven, first thing I'll do
I'll blow my horn and call for blue.

Malinche Mask: Leonora Carrington's Hidden Self-Portrait

A white horse wears my face at dusk. She leaps through
golden curtains, springs for the forest. Dawn horse gone.

A white rocking horse mounted to a blue wall, my choice.
Save for a stiff chair and you, my she-hyena, cold graces my room.

I write this poem from Mexico City, where one day, Mexicans
will bury me under Popocatépetl, soil for a soiled woman.

Two beautiful boy bodies, parted from my womb, are born
to Mexico. Is anything mine to keep, besides my wild brown hair?

My art   my words.
My love   my love?

I glaze over praise, this bit of recognition, this love.
Men who taught me, the first pilgrim   Max.

When the white horse traverses time   I know
this is where I belong. Texcoco, desert lake, mask your cactus face.

I might have been the one indigenous women loath.
Spit her name and air rips like canvas, the portrait I
keep from you. Break or bend time. She is I.
La Malinche soy yo, Leonora, soundless she lion.

Her sex. Is it her fault her legs
Is it her fault her eyes
Is it her fault her sex....

I am Mexican because here I will die.

Pickles

Pickles
or
Yo-Yo Ma?

She dies
slowly.

The master
plays Bach
for his teacher's
wife.

Her wish
his
command.

Waves of round
velvet notes
fill her
bedroom.

But she wants
pickles,
not Bach.

Yo-Yo Ma
storms out.

Returns
an hour later
with nine jars of
pickles.

A Short Line at the Drive-Thru Funeral Home, New Roads, Louisiana

Across the River, paying your respects is easier than

ordering beignets and coffee with chicory.

Thank god for the convenience of drive-thru windows.

First National Bank, long converted to a drive-thru funeral home,

answers an age-old problem with a modern-day solution.

A clerk makes sure the Landrieus are separated from the Morrels,

wheels in the casket with your choice of gospel or jazz.

Sign a register. Take your receipt.

Visiting hours until 5 p.m., 6 p.m. on Thursdays.

Next stop, decide between wedding cake snow

cone or a strawberry daiquiri.

Morning

For our bedroom, I dare find
inspiration in the swan,
two necks in sudden heart shape.

Swans, captured in acrylic, stay silent.
Outside our lover's nest, orange
opens through parted blue curtains.

A smile escapes me every time I
see a swan. I think of how you
hover near me, my constant.

Neither crows nor mindless doves,
doing their noisy high wire act,
care if I survive you.

Red Dies Pretty

A swift swoosh at her ear,
crimson blur falls from a tall water oak.
The hush at her feet is new
plumes and stale-bread bones.

Red dies pretty.

White streaks stained on sky
portend a strange celebration.
Small beaked survivors chatter
over a simple awakening,

the first day of Spring.

Clouds tell their own silent story.
Cotton candy explosions
drowned by indifference.

Yellow rays scent warm air sweet.

When sky favors puffy pale,
shedding winter in New Orleans
is as easy as taking off her coat,
tossing a young beauty in the trash.

No one taught her how to smash
fuzzy feathers, a tender body
between pages of a heavy atlas.

Spring brings but one choice:
to accept another year on this cracked earth.
Her life for the dead cardinal on her porch.

Iron Cross Suite

for Blanca Estela Palacio
December 5, 1949 – June 4, 1994

the passion cross, *la cruz de pasión*

Bless this house with passion.

In memory of me,
don't go out with your hair wet.

You have my blessing to live your life, grow up.

       Why didn't you tell me that before you gasped your last breath?
Don't go out with your hair wet, you'll catch a cold.

Do this in memory of me.

My mother curled her hair at night. She found
a round angle for her black head of soft pink rollers.

I want your straight hair, I'd say.
I want your curls, she'd say.

the dove, *la paloma blanca*

At the top of her iron cross, a white dove
because her name is Blanca.

fleur de lis, *la flor de lis*

Abracadabra p&b sandwiches.
The tips of the iron curl in a fleur de lis, magic with a flourish.

the lightning, *el relámpago*

Lightning bolts scatter to the four cardinal corners.
Meet in infinity or vanish beyond a whisper, the last note of a song.

the balance, *el balance*

At the base of the cross: a Balance, el Balance
Balance is giving equal weight to all aspects of your life.

Do you remember when a lollipop in your mouth was as important as playing
    with the neighborhood kids,
but less than listening to your mother or doing homework?

Balance.

Tell me what is important in your life?
Do you still give equal weight to chocolate and boys?

Talk to me. I hear you, though my life on earth is over.

I live between orange clouds and the moon. My home is shaped like a popsicle.
See my orange cloud when you most need me.

Remember me and I will show you my face on an orange cloud.
Do this in memory of me.

the moon, *la luna*

Late one evening, at the supermarket, the butcher calls me sweetheart.

Sometimes I shop at midnight, when meat
can't deceive and fruit cannot fool you
under obnoxious fluorescent lamps.
Even the aisles of junk food are less tempting during an insomniac's shopping spree.

I stop to wonder...
Was it the Harvest Moon or has the butcher
always been a woman with my mother's voice?

the rooster, *el gallo*

The rooster is perched below the moon on my mother's iron cross.
The rooster sits on the left side because the priest was too late.
Bless me father.... I say the words for her.

Do you deny me?
Do you believe?
Will you come when I need you?

The rooster crows three times.
The rooster because the priest needs more time,
more money, more information, more.

Bring Father Gorman to the hospital.

He is coming.
Hold on another second, another minute, another hour,
hold on, another day.

Never mind he was her favorite priest.
Never mind she gave every penny she could reasonably spare.
Never mind she made a big donation for a new parking lot
to St. Mathias Cathedral on Florence Avenue.

Where is Father Gorman?
He is on HIS way.

Bless me Father for I have sinned.

She ran out of days and breath. Father Gorman never came.

He didn't have time in his priestly schedule to perform the funeral rites.

Have mercy on us. Father, I deny you.

the sun, *el sol*

She is divine.
Three years pass until I can step foot in a church or cathedral.

Remember pain? Forgive. Do this in memory of me.

In the ambulance, my mother was lucid, alert.
She heard the siren's wail in the background.

Time performed its own show,
waited for destiny, its grand finale.

Blanca begged for a piece of paper. She had something important to say.

The scrap of paper might as well have been a discarded candy wrapper,
a school girl's last note tossed to the wind.

Her final words scribbled down.
A maze of plastic tubes kept her from speaking her wisdom.

I unfolded the paper.
The ambulance guy is cute, the note said. The driver is good too.
She managed to scrawl a smiley face, her last signature.

Don't give up. Live.
Do this in memory of me.

Acknowledgments

I WOULD LIKE TO ACKNOWLEDGE the many blessings I've received during the making of this book. My love and thanks goes to Steve Beisner and my family, especially Blanca Estela, Maria Victoria, and Emily. I am grateful to every editor, teacher, student, colleague, and friend who has encouraged my voice. Perie Longo at the Santa Barbara Writers Conference awarded me the 2003 First Prize in Poetry and named me a poet and novelist before I had ever published anything. I appreciate the Community of Writers at Squaw Valley for providing me a scholarship to a glorious poetry residency in 2008. That same year, Quincy Troupe published eight of my poems in Black Renaissance/Renassance Noire. The issue arrived in November for my birthday.

My special gratitude to Arthur Dawson, who chose my first poetry chapbook, *Folsom Lockdown*, as Kulupi Press' Sense of Place 2009 winner. A grant from Poets & Writers helped fund the *Folsom Lockdown* book tour. Nancy Harris gave me my first featured reading in New Orleans at the Maple Leaf Bar; I appreciate her support and friendship.

A heartfelt thanks goes to Katey O'Neill, Beyond Baroque, La Bloga, Reyna Grande, Barry Spacks, David Starkey, Diana Raab, Alicia Partnoy, Mary and Barnaby Conrad, Marcia Meier, Monte Schulz, Nicole Starczak, Mary L. Brown, Toni Lorien, Alison M. Bailey, Sojourner Kincaid Rolle, elena minor, Susan Chiavelli, Daniel Olivas, Michael Sedano, Rafael Alvarado, Pat Minjarez, Lora Martin, Flavia Valle, Luivette Resto, Melanie Leavitt, Stuart Strum, Donna Barros, Susan Larson, Gina Ferrara, Sharon Dirlams, Mary and Eddie Ortega, Gary Young, Denise Chávez, Daniel Zolinsky, Juan Felipe Herrera, and especially to Luis J. Rodriguez, Trini Rodriguez, and all the Tía Chucha Press poets I am honored to join.

"How Fire Is A Story, Waiting" published in *BorderSenses*, *Edible Ojai*, *Maple Leaf Rag III: An Anthology of Poems*, Portals Press, and *La Bloga*.

"Boyhood Bop: B Train," published in *Oranges and Sardines Poets and Artists* and forthcoming in *Bop, Strut, Dance: A Post-Blue Form for New Generations*.

"Porch Days," published in *Black Renaissance/Renaissance Noire*.

"Ramona Street," published in *Black Renaissance/Renaissance Noire Noire* and *Folsom Lockdown*, Kulupi Press.

"El South-Central Cucuy," published in *New Poets of the American West*, Many Voices Press.

"Bozo Takes a Hit for Dad," published in PALABRA: *A Magazine of Chicano & Latino Literary Art* and *Folsom Lockdown*, Kulupi Press.

"Abuela's Higuera," published in *O&S Poets and Artists* and *Folsom Lockdown*, Kulupi Press.

"Dancing with Zorro's Ghost," published in *Black Renaissance/Renaissance Noire* and *Folsom Lockdown*, Kulupi Press.

"Things to Carry," published in *Sage Trail Poetry Magazine* and *Folsom Lockdown*, Kulupi Press.

"Remember Persephone," published in *Homeboy Review* and *Folsom Lockdown*, Kulupi Press.

"Names and Numbers," published in Folsom Lockdown and Pilgrimage Magazine.

"Sister's Shakedown at Steven's Steakhouse," published in PALABRA: *A Magazine of Chicano & Latino Literary Art* and *Folsom Lockdown*, Kulupi Press.

"Día de Independencia/Independence Day," published in *2012 San Diego Poetry Annual*.

"Tea Fire, Santa Barbara 2008," published in *Folsom Lockdown, Kulupi Press*.

"Last Generation of Tourists," published in *Quercus Review*.

"disconcerted crow," published in *Pilgrimage Magazine* and in the anthology *A Bird Black as the Sun: California Poets on Crows and Ravens*.

"Outlaw Zone," published in *2011 San Diego Poetry Annual*, *La Bloga*, and forthcoming in *Poetry of Resistance: A Multi-Cultural Response to AZ SB 1070 and Other Xenophobic Laws*.

"The Framed Virgin," published in *Maple Leaf Rag IV: An Anthology of Poetic Writings New Orleans*, *Folsom Lockdown*, Kulupi Press, and winner of the Santa Barbara Writers Conference Poetry First Prize 2003.

"México Lindo," published in *Black Renaissance/Renaissance Noire*.

"The Blue House," published in *Black Renaissance/Renaissance Noire*.

"Chinaberry Tree on Calle de Parian, Mesilla, New Mexico," published in *Buffalo Carp*.

"Mesilla Sunset," published in *Sage Trail Poetry Magazine*.

"Balloon Fiesta," forthcoming in *200 New Mexico Poems*.

"Sin Vergüenza Swagger," published in *Hinchas de Poesia #5*.

"Quince Jam," published in *Edible Ojai*.

"The Old Mission's Bell," was written for the Creative Community TV channel's special on the Santa Barbara Mission, published in El Tecolote's 40th Anniversary *Revista Literaria de El Tecolote*.

"Chasing Self: Yinka Shonibare & a Flying Machine," was written in response to the Santa Barbara Museum of Art's showcase of Yinka Shonibare's work and for the city's celebration of National Poetry Month 2009.

"Panamanian Percentage," published in *Askew Poetry Journal*.

"Distant Suds," published in *Black Renaissance/Renaissance Noire*.

"En Los Esteikes Senaikes/ In the United Steaks," *2011 San Diego Poetry Annual*.

"Laughter," published in *Black Renaissance/Renaissance Noire* and reprinted on *Kathy Cano-Murillo's Blog*.

"Water Mark," *published in O&S Poets and Artists.*

"Life Beyond the Rio Grande," published in *Black Renaissance/Renaissance Noire.*

"Apology to a New Orleans Tree," published in *Naugatuck River Review.*

"Who Will Pick His Apples," published in *Phati'tude Literary Magazine.*

"Offering to Saint Roch," published in *The Mas Tequila Review* and forthcoming in *The Lives We Seek: Contemporary Poems Inspired by the Saints.*

"The Fisherman and the Evening News," published in *San Pedro River Review* and *Southern Poetry Anthology IV: Louisiana*, Texas Review Press.

"Arroyo Burro Beach," published in *Maple Leaf Rag IV: An Anthology of Poetic Writings New Orleans*, Portals Press.

"Be Bop for Blanca," published in *Bop, Strut, Dance: A Post-Blues Form for New Generations.*

"Choosing a Coffin," published in *Sage Trail Poetry Magazine* and *Folsom Lockdown*, Kulupi Press.

"Abuela's Candle for Saint Jude," published in *Eleven Eleven.*

"Broken Hallelujah," published in *Pilgrimage Magazine.*

"How Else?" published in *PALABRA: A Magazine of Chicano & Latino Literary Art.*

"Etts and Josefina, Sisters on Montezuma Road," published in *Folsom Lockdown*, Kulupi Press.

"Questions for Dad," published in *Homeboy Review* and *Folsom Lockdown*, Kulupi Press.

"Blue Bop for Montezuma," published in the *Squaw Valley Review.*
The Italicized refrain for "Blue Bop for Montezuma" is taken from the lyrics of the folk song *Old Blue.*

"Pickles," published in *Naugatuck River Review*.

"A Short Line at the Drive-Thru Funeral Home, New Roads, Louisiana," published in *The Mas Tequila Review.*

"Iron Cross Suite," was written for the art exhibit, Forged in Iron: The Expressive Art of the Roof Top Tradition in Chiapas, Mexico, shown at Casa de la Guerra, Santa Barbara, CA.